Holiness of Heart and Life: Loving God and Neighbor

Allan R. Bever

Topical Line Drives
#49

Energion Publications
Gonzalez, Florida
2023

ISBN: 978-1-63199-852-2
eISBN: 978-1-63199-853-9

Energion Publications
P. O. Box 841
Gonzalez, FL 32560

For all the great saints I have served as pastor
from 1984 through 2022.
They have embodied for me holiness of heart and life.

TABLE OF CONTENTS

1. Introduction: Why Holiness?   1
2. What Holiness Is Not   7
    Holiness is Not Legalism 7
    Holiness is Not Majoring in the Minors   10
    Holiness is Not Self-Righteous   12
    Holiness Is Not About Appeasing God   15
3. Holiness is Loving God   17
    The Shema   17
    Jeremiah—Obedience to the Law as Second Nature 19
    The Symbolic as Reminder   21
4. Holiness Is Loving Neighbor   22
    Amos—Ethical Monotheism   22
    The Good Samaritan—Loving Every Neighbor   24
    James and John—Loving Neighbor Because of Love for God 26
5. Going on to Perfection or The Pursuit of Holiness Today 28
    Holiness—Delighting in the Amazing Love of God   28
    Holiness on the Ground   30
    The General Rules   30
6. Discipleship in the Current Age   34
7. Conclusion: Holiness is Irresistible   36

1. Introduction: Why Holiness?

Holiness is not a fashionable word in the church today. All too often when the term is uttered people hear "holier-than-thou," a judgmental form of Christianity that looks down on others who don't measure up to a certain form of legalism. The Holier-Than-Thou individual turns following Jesus into drudgery focusing on just following the rules, many of those rules being trivial—as the old saying goes, "I don't drink, smoke, or chew nor go with folks who do." We will highlight what holiness is not in the next chapter, but suffice it to say that what it means to pursue holiness is often misunderstood or caricatured into something negative.

It is difficult to read the Bible without seeing that holiness is a major theme in both the Old and New Testaments. In the Old Testament, the word "holiness" (Hebrew; *qādôš*) is found 431 times. In the New Testament, the word (Greek; *hagios*) is used 200 times. Without even looking at the specific contexts of these two terms, it is clear that holiness is a concern of the biblical writers. Indeed, I suggest that holiness is not only important for Christians; it is required. The journey of following Jesus is impossible without the pursuit of holiness.

This number of occurrences of the word throughout Scripture in and of itself should be adequate to convince people that holiness is important for believers, but those negative connotations associated with the word are so ingrained in people that more of an explanation is needed. So, why holiness?

First, holiness is necessary because God is holy. Holiness is an essential characteristic of God's being, of who God is. When Moses stands before the burning bush, the voice of God commands him, "'Come no closer! Remove the sandals from your feet, for the place on which you are standing is holy ground'" (Exodus 3:5). God doesn't just demonstrate holiness in God's actions, God's very being is holy. The Prophet Isaiah has a vision of God in the Temple:

> In the year that King Uzziah died, I saw the Lord sitting on a throne, high and lofty; and the hem of his robe filled the temple. Seraphs were in attendance above him; each had six wings: with two they covered their faces, and with two they

covered their feet, and with two they flew. And one called to another and said:

'Holy, holy, holy is the LORD of hosts;
the whole earth is full of his glory" (Isaiah 6:1-3).

That God is holy means that God is other than creation. While God is present in creation, God must not be confused with creation. To make the Creator intrinsic to creation itself is idolatry (Romans 1:18-23). The ancient Hebrews drew such a sharp line between God and the world that it was forbidden to portray the God of Israel with any imagery—a sculpture or a painting. This was so important that the prohibition of not fashioning idols of any kind worked its way into the Ten Commandments (Exodus 20:4; Deuteronomy 5:8) which formed the foundation of all the bylaws given in the Torah (the ancient rabbis counted 613). This did not mean that God was separated from the world, but that the distinction between creator and creation was emphasized. It was the portrayal of deities in forms that blurred the distinction.

God's uniqueness from creation reveals God's majesty in creation. God's holiness demonstrates, as the praise chorus says, "Our God is an awesome God."[1] Jacob's dream of a staircase connected from heaven to earth was interpreted by him as an "awesome place" (Genesis 28:17; NRSV). The sole exceptionality of God means that experiencing God in the world leads to a sense of awe and wonder, but it is also the case that the experience of the divine presence can lead to terror, not because God is scary, but rather because the realization of God's holiness reveals human imperfection and sin. Isaiah's vision of God in the temple causes him to proclaim, "'Woe is me! I am lost, for I am a man of unclean lips, and I live among a people of unclean lips'" (Isaiah 6:5). The psalmist admonishes, "Worship the LORD in holy splendor; tremble before him, all the earth (Psalm 96:9). No human beings in their sin can experience the fullness of God's holy presence "the very face of God," and live.

Moses said to the LORD, 'See, you have said to me, "Bring up this people"; but you have not let me know whom you will send with me. Yet you have said, "I know you by name, and you have also found favor in my sight." *Now if I have found*

---

1 Rich Mullin, BMG Songs, Inc., 1988.

favor in your sight, show me your ways, so that I may know you and find favor in your sight. Consider too that this nation is your people.' He said, 'My presence will go with you, and I will give you rest.' *And he said to him, 'If your presence will not go, do not carry us up from here.* For how shall it be known that I have found favor in your sight, I and your people, unless you go with us? In this way, we shall be distinct, I and your people, from every people on the face of the earth.'

The LORD said to Moses, 'I will do the very thing that you have asked; for you have found favor in my sight, and I know you by name.' *Moses said, 'Show me your glory, I pray.'* And he said, 'I will make all my goodness pass before you, and will proclaim before you the name, "The LORD"; and I will be gracious to whom I will be gracious, and will show mercy on whom I will show mercy. *But', he said, 'you cannot see my face; for no one shall see me and live.' And the LORD continued, 'See, there is a place by me where you shall stand on the rock; and while my glory passes by I will put you in a cleft of the rock, and I will cover you with my hand until I have passed by; then I will take away my hand, and you shall see my back; but my face shall not be seen.'* (Exodus 33:12-33; italics are my emphasis).

And when God passes by Elijah at Mount Horeb, the prophet covers his face with his mantle knowing he is in the presence of divine holiness (1 Kings 19:11-13)

Everything in creation that is associated with God is holy. God makes things holy. When the people of Israel come together in God's presence, it is called "a holy assembly" (Exodus 12:16) On the Sabbath when worshipers gather to enter the presence of God, it is "a holy Sabbath" (Exodus 16:23). Zion is God's holy mountain (Psalm 2:6), and God's throne in heaven is holy (Psalm 47:8). Above all, God's name is holy and shall not be taken in vain or spoken in cheap and profane ways (Exodus 20:7; Deuteronomy 5:11).

God's holiness has clear implications for God's people. "For I am the LORD your God; sanctify yourselves therefore, and be holy, for I am holy (Leviticus 11:44; see also 1 Peter 1:16). As God is set apart from creation, so God's people Israel in the Old Testament are to be set apart from the other nations of the world. They do that by reflecting the holy ways of God in the world. "For you are a people holy to the LORD your God; the LORD your God has chosen you out of all the peoples on earth to be his people, his treasured possession" (Deuteronomy 7:6). Such set apartness does not mean isolation from the other nations; it means a way of life as an alternative to the nations. In their holiness God's people demonstrate their set apart ways to bear witness to the set apartness of the one true God of Israel in contrast to the false gods of their neighbors. Such holiness becomes an invitation to the nations to worship the God of Israel, to enter into God's presence that they too may be taught the ways of God.

> In days to come
> the mountain of the LORD's house
> shall be established as the highest of the mountains,
> and shall be raised above the hills;
> all the nations shall stream to it.
> Many peoples shall come and say,
> 'Come, let us go up to the mountain of the LORD,
> to the house of the God of Jacob;
> that he may teach us his ways
> and that we may walk in his paths' (Isaiah 2:2-3).

The New Testament not only affirms the essential holiness of God (Mark 1:24; John 6:69; 14:11), but it reinforces the necessity that God's people, the church, be holy as well. As Israel in the Old Testament is to be a holy nation, so is the church in the New Testament. "But you are a chosen race, a royal priesthood, a holy nation, God's own people, in order that you may proclaim the mighty acts of him who called you out of darkness into his marvelous light" (1 Peter 2:9). It is in the work of Jesus Christ on the cross, that the church is made holy (Hebrews 10:10). The Sermon on the Mount in Matthew (Chapters 5-7), which in some ways functions as a summary of Jesus' kingdom ethic, is a call to holiness. Jesus admonishes his hears to "be perfect, therefore, as your heavenly Father is perfect" (5:48).

The Apostle Paul focuses on holiness as the transformation of the total person (1 Thessalonians 5:23) through faith in Christ and the power of the Holy Spirit. Paul often refers to the recipients of his letters as "saints," "holy ones" (e.g. Romans 1:7; 1 Corinthians

1:2; 2 Corinthians 1:1; Philippians 1:1) who are called and set apart for the gospel. It is Jesus Christ "who became for us wisdom from God, and righteousness and sanctification" [i.e. holiness] "and redemption" (1 Corinthians 1:30); and it is the Holy Spirit that enlivens the work of Christ in the life of the believers. "Since we live by the Spirit, let us also be guided by the Spirit (Galatians 5:25).

It should now be obvious that the answer to the question of the importance of holiness is answered by Scripture. The pursuit of holiness is necessary for God's people. The problem, however, as was stated at the beginning of this introduction, is that too often what passes for holiness in the church today does not look like the holiness we see in the Bible. Too many believers have experienced *in the* church, and too many unbelievers have experienced *from the* church a harmful form of "holiness" that is toxic, hurtful, and unlike divine holiness. Such toxicity too often pushes people away from God instead of fulfilling the vision of Isaiah 2:2-3 where the nations gladly come to the mountain of the Lord that the holy ways of God may be taught to all the world.

How true it is that sometimes in order to understand the true character of something, we first have to tear away the false caricatures that hide the actual reality. This is the case with holiness. Thus, in the next chapter we will embark on a mission of caricature killing in the hope that the life-giving nature of holiness will once again sparkle from the Mountain of Zion.

2. What Holiness Is Not

Sometimes beliefs and ideas get a bad reputation, not for what they are, but in how they have been mischaracterized. When I was a boy, we were not allowed to use poker cards because they had become so associated with gambling, which my parents were against, that we had to play card games using other kinds of cards—Old Maid, Uno, Go Fish. Even though my brother and I didn't gamble (what can a child gamble away), we were not allowed to play with poker cards because they were guilty by association.

That's the problem with holiness. It has been associated with several unpleasant and negative things, that when people hear the word, they cringe. So, before we can discuss what holiness is, we must be clear as to what holiness is not.

Holiness is Not Legalism

Legalism has been defined in various ways. I think of legalism as making the law an end in and of itself. The law at its best is a means to an end. The end of the law depends on what specific code we are talking about. Secular law is at its best when it is employed as a means to human flourishing. The Torah (the Law of Moses) is at its best when it is employed to reveal Israel to the nations as God's people who shine a light to the rest of the world what God expects. What does God expect? Micah 6:8 states it specifically.

> He has told you, O mortal, what is good;
>   and what does the Lord require of you
> but to do justice, and to love kindness,
>   and to walk humbly with your God?

But once the law is no longer a means to an end, but the end in and of itself, holiness becomes legalism. When the law is employed legalistically, it no longer exists for people; it exists for its own sake.

The legalist's favorite phrase when it comes to enforcing the rules is, "But it's the law!" There can be no room for considering the circumstances that led to the infraction, no analysis of the particular situation. The law is the end. All who break the same law are equally guilty and subject to the exact same penalty.

In 2005, in the aftermath of Hurricane Katrina that brought much loss of life and destruction to the Gulf Coast and the city of New Orleans, helicopters caught footage of people taking advantage of the situation to loot. Overhead, individuals could be seen carrying away televisions and computers and anything else they could carry. And yet, there were others, desperate to feed their families who took food from the abandoned local grocery stores in order to feed their hungry children. Did all break the law? Yes. Were the motivations and circumstances different? Yes. Should a judge deal with the mother just trying to feed her children in the same way as the man who wanted a new flatscreen TV? The legalist would say, "Yes! It's the law!" There can be no mercy for the mom who couldn't bear the cries of her hungry children.

What about immigrants who enter the country illegally? They come to the United States looking for a better life. After they get here, they have children who are growing up in the only country they have known. The parents' illegal status has been discovered. Should they be returned to their home country taking them away from their children who are left to live in their country of birth away from mom and dad? Should the law treat them differently from the illegal immigrant who came to this country to sell drugs and traffic in human beings? The legalist would say, "Yes! It's the law!" The legalist might say they feel badly, but the law is the law. If one person is given leniency, then the force of the law is undermined.

Jesus did not get along well with the legalists. Contrary to much Protestant interpretation of the New Testament, the religious leaders in Jesus' day were not legalists in that they believed the law earned one salvation. Just as Jesus, the Pharisees believed salvation was a gift. The legalism of the Pharisees in reality was how they viewed the implementation of the law. The law was the end in and of itself. It was to be administered strictly without regard to circumstances.

Jesus chastises his contemporaries for this perspective. On several occasions, Jesus heals on the Sabbath provoking the charge from the Pharisees that he violated the Sabbath by doing work.

On another occasion, Jesus and his disciples glean from the field (Leviticus 23:22) on the Sabbath because they were hungry.

> One sabbath he was going through the cornfields; and as they made their way his disciples began to pluck heads of grain. The Pharisees said to him, 'Look, why are they doing what is not lawful on the sabbath?' And he said to them, 'Have you never read what David did when he and his companions were hungry and in need of food? He entered the house of God, when Abiathar was high priest, and ate the bread of the Presence, which it is not lawful for any but the priests to eat, and he gave some to his companions.' Then he said to them, 'The sabbath was made for humankind, and not humankind for the sabbath; so the Son of Man is lord even of the sabbath' (Mark 2:23-28).

Notice Jesus' criticism. "The sabbath was made for humankind, and not humankind for the sabbath." The sabbath was given as a means to an end; the end was the flourishing of God's people. Once a week the people were to take a day and rest from their labors. They were to worship and enjoy time with family. It was a time to remember that life was not reduced to toil, but was given for enjoyment. Life and its pleasures were a divine gift. The Pharisees had turned Sabbath into the end. Human beings were no longer the focus of that holy day, the focus was the day itself. Sabbath observance had turned into the very toil it was meant to avoid. Scot McKnight says that the difference between Jesus' view of the law and the Pharisees was that while the Pharisees taught the love of Torah, Jesus taught the Torah of love.[2]

Jesus reminded the religious leaders that they too took into account extenuating circumstances in keeping the law.

> On one occasion when Jesus was going to the house of a leader of the Pharisees to eat a meal on the sabbath, they were watching him closely. Just then, in front of him, there was a man who had dropsy. And Jesus asked the lawyers and Pharisees, 'Is it lawful to cure people on the sabbath, or not?' But they were silent. So Jesus took him and healed him, and

---

2 Scot McKnight, *Kingdom Conspiracy: Returning to the Radical Mission of the Local Church* (Grand Rapids: Brazos Press, 2014), p. 51.

sent him away. Then he said to them, 'If one of you has a child or an ox that has fallen into a well, will you not immediately pull it out on a sabbath day?' And they could not reply to this (Luke 14:1-6).

Legalism may have the appearance of holiness but falls far short of the kind of holiness the Bible requires. God gave the law, not as an end but as a means to an end—Holiness requires not the love of the law, but the law of love. Legalism dehumanizes the lawbreaker, something Jesus never did.

To reject legalism is not to embrace antinomianism—the rejection of the law itself. The law matters. The law is necessary. God's giving of the law was an act of grace and a demonstration of divine mercy. When grace and mercy are removed from the law, it no longer serves its purpose. Legalism takes the law given in grace and mercy and implements it without the mercy and grace necessary for its fulfillment.

Holiness is not legalism.

HOLINESS IS NOT MAJORING IN THE MINORS

In the 1993 film *Gettysburg*,[3] the actor playing Confederate General James Kemper says to General George Pickett, "Well, I got to hand it to you, George. You sure got a talent for trivializing the momentous and complicating the obvious. You ever consider running for Congress?"

The truth of the matter is that it's not just Congress that trivializes the momentous. All human beings have such a talent. In trivializing the momentous, we also often make mountains out of molehills, that is, we major in minors.

In the Introduction, I spoke of not being allowed to play with poker cards as a boy because they were closely associated with gambling. The justifiable major concern of gambling was transferred to the playing cards themselves. The result was majoring in a minor—putting undo focus on the wrong and trivial thing.

I think it is often the case that we major in minors for two reasons; First, we find that the truly important aspects of the law are

---

3 https://www.imdb.com/title/tt0107007/

too difficult to follow. Therefore, secondarily we turn our attention to the small things associated with the big thing. That allows us to obey the minutiae deceiving ourselves into following the rules, while ignoring the truly significant principles of the law we find too difficult to keep. In Matthew 23, Jesus accuses the religious leaders of this very thing:

> 'Woe to you, blind guides, who say, "Whoever swears by the sanctuary is bound by nothing, but whoever swears by the gold of the sanctuary is bound by the oath." You blind fools! For which is greater, the gold or the sanctuary that has made the gold sacred? And you say, "Whoever swears by the altar is bound by nothing, but whoever swears by the gift that is on the altar is bound by the oath." How blind you are! For which is greater, the gift or the altar that makes the gift sacred? So whoever swears by the altar, swears by it and by everything on it; and whoever swears by the sanctuary, swears by it and by the one who dwells in it; and whoever swears by heaven, swears by the throne of God and by the one who is seated upon it.
> 'Woe to you, scribes and Pharisees, hypocrites! For you tithe mint, dill, and cummin, and have neglected the weightier matters of the law: justice and mercy and faith. It is these you ought to have practiced without neglecting the others. You blind guides! You strain out a gnat but swallow a camel! (Matthew 23:16-24)

In referring to the weightier matters of the law, Jesus reminds us again of Micah 6:8—we are to act *justly*, to love *mercy*, and to *walk humbly* with God. The dilemma we confront is all too often fulfilling Micah 6:8 in our lives calls for sacrifice; it can also be complicated. Life itself can be complicated. How do we seek justice for those who are victimized by racism? How do we offer mercy to the drug dealer or the pimp? How do we walk humbly and faithfully with God by associating with those of questionable character?

We find it easier to ignore the complexities by disregarding the problem offering instead simplistic solutions—we major in the minors. Racism isn't embedded in the culture, it's just a few bad apples. Those who commit crimes just need to be locked up. They are beyond help. We can't associate with bad people, addicts, and prostitutes. They will damage our reputations.

In reducing faithfulness to simplistic and easy solutions we treat the law and the great principles the law embodies as trivial matters. In order to avoid the commitment required to fulfill the law we do exactly what the Pharisees did—we strain out a gnat and swallow a camel.

Holiness is not majoring in the minors.

HOLINESS IS NOT SELF-RIGHTEOUS

The one attitude that turns most people off to the idea of holiness is the "holier-than-thou" attitude. Such individuals come off as being morally better than everyone else. They not only act superior; they have no trouble pointing out the faults of others. Even a superficial reading of the Gospels demonstrates Jesus' was also turned off by the holier-than-thou crowd.

In Luke 18:9-14 we are read that Jesus

> told this parable to some who trusted in themselves that they were righteous and regarded others with contempt: 'Two men went up to the temple to pray, one a Pharisee and the other a tax-collector. The Pharisee, standing by himself, was praying thus, "God, I thank you that I am not like other people: thieves, rogues, adulterers, or even like this tax-collector. I fast twice a week; I give a tenth of all my income." But the tax-collector, standing far off, would not even look up to heaven, but was beating his breast and saying, "God, be merciful to me, a sinner!" I tell you, this man went down to his home justified rather than the other; for all who exalt themselves will be humbled, but all who humble themselves will be exalted.'

We miss the punch of this parable if we cast the Pharisee as the hypocrite and the tax-collector as the poor righteous soul trying to do his best. What the Pharisee and the tax collector say about themselves is true.

The Pharisees were indeed the righteous men of their day. Jesus tangled with the Pharisaic leadership and their hypocrisy, but there were many other Pharisees who were no doubt faithful to God and their Jewish faith. When the Pharisee is in the Temple giving to God his litany of self-kudos, he is telling the truth. He does fast twice a week. He tithes. It is also the case that he is not like the other people he mentions. He is not a thief or a rogue, an adulterer, nor a tax collector. He is not lying. He is telling the truth.

This Pharisee is the kind of person who you want as your next-door neighbor. He's a great guy. He will bring you chicken soup when you're sick. He will watch your house while you are away on vacation. You can trust him alone with your children. Fathers—you want this kind of guy to marry your daughter!

The tax collector, on the other hand, is not like the Pharisee. He is a good-for-nothing crook. When the Romans wanted to collect taxes from one of their subject peoples, they employed as tax collectors people native to the land. The Romans knew it would be easier to collect taxes if they could get subjects to collect from subjects. So, in order to collect taxes from the Jews, they employed Jews to collect the tax. The Romans did not pay tax collectors a wage. A tax collector's money was made by what he could get from people over and above the tax each individual owed. In order to get money above the required tax, tax collectors often collaborated with Roman soldiers who would accompany the collector to an individual house in order to "shake down" the residents. The tax collector would then give the soldiers their "cut" and the tax collector would go home with a rather hefty profit.

In Israel the people hated tax collectors for two reasons: they collaborated with Roman soldiers to steal from their own people, and by working for the Romans to collect the tax for a foreign power, they were traitors.

You do not want this tax collector for a next-door neighbor. Don't count on him bringing you chicken soup when you're sick. When you leave town, you will have to get one person to watch your house, and one person to watch him. You would tell your children not to go near him, and Fathers—you dread the day your daughter brings him over "just to meet the family."

Unlike the Pharisee he has nothing good to say about himself, and in that, at least, he is honest. Standing in the Temple he does not even attempt to look up to heaven. He does not thank God with open hands. They are too dirty with corruption to open toward God. He pounds on his chest, and it is too bad he didn't pound harder. He cries out before God, "Be merciful to me a sinner." Like the Pharisee, he has uttered the truth about himself. He is a sinner. He is a sinner before God, before the people of Israel, before the Law of Moses and before himself. If anyone can still be merciful to him, it can only be God.

The problem here is not the hypocrisy of the Pharisee; it is that he believes his righteousness puts him on a moral level above the tax collector. He trusts in his own righteousness and not the righteousness of God who does the work of holiness in his life.

True holiness engenders in us the opposite of self-righteousness. Holiness forms in individuals an attitude of humility. Indeed, the universal testimony of those persons we call saints is that the closer they get to God, the more holy they become, the more intense is the reality of their sin. The great irony of holiness is the more holy a person is, the closer she is to God, and therefore the less holy she feels in the divine presence. True holiness leads to humility, not a feeling of superiority over others. It is holy humility that increases the grace offered to others. Contempt for others is not a hallmark of holiness. The truly holy person heeds the words of Jesus in the Sermon on the Mount:

> 'Do not judge, so that you may not be judged. For with the judgment you make you will be judged, and the measure you give will be the measure you get. Why do you see the speck in your neighbor's eye, but do not notice the log in your own eye? Or how can you say to your neighbor, "Let me take the speck out of your eye", while the log is in your own eye? You hypocrite, first take the log out of your own eye, and then you will see clearly to take the speck out of your neighbor's eye' (Matthew 7:1-5).

Holiness is not self-righteousness.

HOLINESS IS NOT ABOUT APPEASING GOD

The holier-than-thou attitude is not the only thing that turns people off in reference to Christianity. Another attitude is that God is vengefully watching us, waiting for us to slip up in order to judge us. Unfortunately, there is a pop theology in the culture that when we are being obedient to God, life goes well. When we are disobedient, things go badly. In this view of God, suffering and calamity are the result of our sin and God is judging us.

It is certainly the case that we human beings in our bad behavior can bring suffering upon ourselves. Someone drinks too much one evening and suffers the self-inflicted pain of a terrible hangover the next morning. Another person ends up in jail for embezzling money. It is also true that our disobedience can bring suffering upon others. That person who gets drunk decides to drive home and crashes headlong into another car killing a young woman. The individual who embezzled money goes to jail leaving his wife and children to pick up the pieces of their lives. It is true that we bring judgment upon ourselves because of sin.

There is a difference between believing that we can bring judgment upon ourselves for our errant ways, and that God is bringing judgment upon us for our disobedience. The Apostle Paul indicates in the Book of Romans that God's judgment is not activity on God's part, but of humanity going its own way disregarding God's law (Romans 1:18-32). In failing to live in God's will we reap the consequences of our own actions.

However, that does not fully explain suffering and calamity. There is suffering that just happens because of the world we live in. It cannot be ascribed to God or our actions.

3. Holiness is Loving God

In order to understand holiness, we must know that it is inextricably tied to love. Holiness is our loving response to the God who loves us. This holy response can be seen throughout the Bible from beginning to end. Indeed, there is a narrative thread of holy love that runs through Scripture. If we are to love God, we must also love our neighbor. Those two cannot be separated. For the sake of our discussion, however, we will focus on each in turn, but first we lay the foundation for holy love by looking at the foundational statement of Jewish belief and practice—the Shema found in Deuteronomy 6:4-9.

THE SHEMA

The name of this passage of Scripture is derived from the Hebrew word "to hear." While the beginning focus is often on verse four, it should be noted that this section of Deuteronomy actually starts at verse one. With that in mind I now quote verses 1-9, but will italicize beginning in verse six.

> Now this is the commandment—the statutes and the ordinances—that the LORD your God charged me to teach you to observe in the land that you are about to cross into and occupy, so that you and your children and your children's children may fear the LORD your God all the days of your life, and keep all his decrees and his commandments that I am commanding you, so that your days may be long. Hear therefore, O Israel, and observe them diligently, so that it may go well with you, and so that you may multiply greatly in a land flowing with milk and honey, as the LORD, the God of your ancestors, has promised you.
>
> *Hear, O Israel: The LORD is our God, the LORD alone. You shall love the LORD your God with all your heart, and with all your soul, and with all your might. Keep these words that I am commanding you today in your heart. Recite them to your children and talk about them when you are at home and when you are away, when you lie down and when you rise. Bind them as a sign on your hand, fix them as an emblem on your forehead, and write them on the doorposts of your house and on your gates.*

The Shema is the foundation of Israel's covenant with God. It affirms that there is only one God and that God's people are to be faithful to that one God to the exclusion of all others. For many centuries, the Shema has been recited as a daily prayer along with Deuteronomy 11:13-21 and Numbers 15:37-41. The Hebrew words translated by the NRSV as "The LORD is our God, the LORD alone," literally read, "Yahweh, our God, Yahweh one."[4] This is not a declaration that the God of Israel is to be worshiped and revered as the first among other deities as was commonplace in the ancient Near Eastern world, but exclusively as the only God who rules over all things. The God of Abraham, Isaac, and Jacob had no rivals. There is only one God and that God is a unity.[5] Jesus himself affirmed the loving of God as the greatest commandment.

> One of the scribes came near and heard them disputing with one another, and seeing that he answered them well, he asked him, 'Which commandment is the first of all?' Jesus answered, 'The first is, "Hear, O Israel: the Lord our God, the Lord is one; you shall love the Lord your God with all your heart, and with all your soul, and with all your mind, and with all your strength." The second is this, "You shall love your neighbor as yourself." There is no other commandment greater than these' (Mark 12:28-31)

God was not only to be worshiped exclusively, but the people of Israel were to reserve themselves and their obedience only to that God, "You shall love the LORD your God with all your heart, and with all your soul, and with all your might" (6:5). For the Hebrews, the heart was the center of reason, equivalent to the mind. The people were to think on the Lord's commands and ponder them in order to live according to their admonitions. The word rendered "soul" can refer to one's being, the vitality of one's existence. Israel was to love God with their entire existence. We might say today that they were to love God from the bottom of their heart. They were to love the Lord their God with everything they had and everything

---

4 J.A. Thompson, *Deuteronomy: An Introduction and Commentary.* D.J. Wiseman, ed. (Downers Grove: InterVarsity Press, 1974), p. 212.
5 Peter C. Craigie, *The Book of Deuteronomy.* The New International Commentary on the Old Testament (Grand Rapids: Eerdmans, 1976), p. 169.

they were and in everything they did. Their love for God was not just a legalism in which God's people did just what was required of them to be acceptable. This was not a transactional relationship. It was a deep love given in return for God's unfathomable love to them.

In keeping God's word, they were loving God with their whole being. In turn, they were to pass those commandments onto their children that they might also love God in the same exclusive way. "Recite them to your children and talk about them when you are at home and when you are away, when you lie down and when you rise" (6:7). Here is education by saturation. Teaching the divine ways was not to be reduced to a small slice of time set aside for such instruction, but it was to permeate all of life that children would come to know that they were first and foremost the children of Israel at every moment of the day, and that God's commands were to be integrated into even the smallest aspects of daily living. The teaching and conversation were to begin at daybreak and continue at every opportune moment until its end. Only in this way would it be possible for future generations to have the law in their hearts and respond in love to God.

JEREMIAH—OBEDIENCE TO THE LAW AS SECOND NATURE

Some 600 years after Moses, the Prophet Jeremiah envisioned a time when such heartfelt devotion will be commonplace among the people.

> The days are surely coming, says the LORD, when I will make a new covenant with the house of Israel and the house of Judah. It will not be like the covenant that I made with their ancestors when I took them by the hand to bring them out of the land of Egypt—a covenant that they broke, though I was their husband, says the LORD. But this is the covenant that I will make with the house of Israel after those days, says the LORD: I will put my law within them, and I will write it on their hearts; and I will be their God, and they shall be my people. No longer shall they teach one another, or say to each other, 'Know the LORD', for they shall all know me, from the least of them to the greatest, says the LORD; for I will for-

give their iniquity, and remember their sin no more (Jeremiah 31:31-34).

It would be wrong to interpret Jeremiah in such a way that a heart-felt obedience to the Lord's commands was something only for the future. As we have seen, the Shema commands God's people to love God with heart, mind, soul, and strength. That God's people often fell short of that dynamic relationship with God and fell into a "going through the motions" or "jumping through the hoops" approach to the law (which often led to disobedience of that law) did not mean that such piety and practice were reserved for a later time. What Jeremiah does foresee in verse 34 is a time when the relationship between God and God's people will be so close and intimate that intermediaries such as priests and even parents will no longer be necessary to instruct others to "know the Lord." They will be in tune with each other and know each other's hearts and minds.[6] We might say today that God and God's people will be in sync. In the meantime, however, the words of Deuteronomy 6 must be heeded—God's people are to teach and demonstrate to future generations how to love God by forming a desire to keep God's ways. Gratitude and devotion can be taught as what is imparted is internalized.

THE SYMBOLIC AS REMINDER

The Shema continues: "Bind them as a sign on your hand, fix them as an emblem on your forehead, and write them on the doorposts of your house and on your gates" (6:8). It is difficult to know if these words were originally meant to be taken literally, but many of Jesus' contemporaries did by binding phylacteries or small boxes (normally on the left arm and forehead) containing a parchment on which various verses were written. (cf. Matthew 23:5). Such boxes (called *Mezuzahs* in Hebrew) were found at Qumran where the Dead Sea Scrolls were discovered.[7]

---

6 J.A. Thompson, *The Book of Jeremiah*. The New International Commentary on the Old Testament (Grand Rapids: Eerdmans, 1980), p. 581.

7 H.L. Ellison, "Phylacteries," *The New Bible Dictionary*. (Downers Grove: Intervarsity Press, 1979), p. 995.

Jesus's criticism of the Pharisees in Matthew 23 did not appear to be directed at such symbolic displays in and of themselves, but rather when the outward display failed to testify to the inward devotion. Today we may display symbols of devotion in our homes such as a plaque of the Ten Commandments or a pictorial representation of Jesus. In and of themselves these are acceptable things to do. They remind us of our faith and the need for faithfulness. However, we become hypocrites when what we display in our homes publicly for people to see is something completely different from how we live. It is reminiscent of my college days many years ago when I honked my horn at a driver in front of me who had a "Honk If You Love Jesus," bumper sticker displayed on his trunk. After I blew my horn, the driver rolled down his window and gave me the finger. What was being said (displayed) and what was actually done were two different things. It was the failure to demonstrate in actions the words proclaimed that angered Jesus (Matthew 23:23-24).

The Shema commands us to love God in our devotion to God—knowing scripture, offering prayers, and worship—corporately and individually. However, the vertical loving of God is not the love God desires if it excludes the horizontal love of neighbor. We see that throughout the Old and New Testaments. To that we now turn.

4. Holiness Is Loving Neighbor

It is impossible to read the stipulations of the law of Moses in Deuteronomy and miss the obligations toward the neighbor God expects of God's people. In fact, one cannot love God rightly without love of neighbor. The connection between the two is so intertwined throughout the Old Testament that the connection is just assumed. In the New Testament the connection between the two is made explicit.

Amos—Ethical Monotheism

The Prophet Amos, whose ministry covered the first half of the eighth century BCE, affirms the covenant tradition rooted in the Shema proclaiming what has generally been called ethical monotheism—serving the one God of Israel requires ethical behavior toward others.[8] Amos targets his message toward the rich and privileged who oppress the poor and who sell the powerless into slavery (2:6-8; 5:11 6:3-6). He is harshly critical of those who have posh summer and winter homes living in luxury while bribing judges to rule against the poor in court (3:15; 4:1; 5:12; 6:4-6).

The greatest indictment against Israel comes in 5:21-24:

> I hate, I despise your festivals,
>   and I take no delight in your solemn assemblies.
> Even though you offer me your burnt-offerings
>   and grain-offerings,
>   I will not accept them;
> and the offerings of well-being of your fatted animals
>   I will not look upon.
> Take away from me the noise of your songs;
>   I will not listen to the melody of your harps.
> But let justice roll down like waters,
>   and righteousness like an ever-flowing stream.

Israel's outward show of piety, which was supposed to be a demonstration of their love for God was in actuality something

---

8 William La Sor, David Hubbard, and Frederic Bush, *Old Testament Survey: The Message, Form, and Background of the Old Testament.* (Grand Rapids: Eerdmans, 1982), p. 123.

that made God sick. Why? Quite simply, their vertical offerings to Yahweh in worship and prayer and sacrifice were hollow and hypocritical because they failed to practice ethical monotheism, that is, they had not demonstrated love for their neighbors. In fact, their behavior demonstrated their contempt for the less fortunate in their midst. Eugene Peterson's translation of this passage gives it a contemporary feel.

> "I can't stand your religious meetings. I'm fed up with your conferences and conventions. I want nothing to do with your religion projects, your pretentious slogans and goals. I'm sick of your fund-raising schemes, your public relations and image making. I've had all I can take of your noisy ego-music. When was the last time you sang to me? Do you know what I want? I want justice - oceans of it. I want fairness - rivers of it. That's what I want. That's all I want.[9]

The Israelites had contented themselves with their Sabbath worship of God as what was required of them alone to be lovers of God. As a result, God saw their worship as nothing more than hollow commotion. What they professed on the Sabbath was ignored during the week. Today, we might say the people of Israel were "Saturday sinners, but Sunday saints." Amos' audience had separated their love of God from love of neighbor. In so doing they loved neither their neighbor nor God. Responding to God's mercy meant securing justice for the neighbor. James Limburg notes,

> God's people doing justice is like a farmer's vineyard producing grapes. Doing justice is the people of God responding to what God has done for them. This pattern of divine indicative followed by expected human response runs through the Bible.[10]

The Prophet Micah will later write, "He has told you, O mortal, what is good; and what does the LORD require of you but to do justice, and to love mercy, and to walk humbly with your God?"

9 Eugene Peterson, *The Message*, accessed www.biblegateway.com (https://www.biblegateway.com/passage/?search=Amos+5%3A21-24&version=MSG).
10 James Limburg, *Hosea-Micah. Interpretation: A Bible Commentary for Teaching and Preaching.* (Atlanta: John Knox Press, 1988), p. 107.

(Micah 6:8). The people of Amos' day believed it was possible to walk humbly with God without doing justice or embracing mercy. Their lack of obedience to the covenant on the horizontal level meant that their vertical devotion to God was more theatrical sham than truthful expression.

THE GOOD SAMARITAN—LOVING EVERY NEIGHBOR

In the last chapter, I quoted Jesus' words concerning the greatest commandment from Mark 12:28-31. I now quote from Luke's version for two major reasons, which I shall explain below.

> Just then a lawyer stood up to test Jesus. 'Teacher,' he said, 'what must I do to inherit eternal life?' He said to him, 'What is written in the law? What do you read there?' He answered, 'You shall love the Lord your God with all your heart, and with all your soul, and with all your strength, and with all your mind; and your neighbor as yourself.' And he said to him, 'You have given the right answer; do this, and you will live' (Luke 10:25-28).

The first major reason is that it should not be missed that in Mark's account, Jesus is the one who quotes the Shema and then adds Leviticus 19:18, "You shall love your neighbor as yourself." Here in Luke, it is the lawyer answering Jesus' question concerning how to inherit eternity who includes both the commands to love God and neighbor. This is important on two accounts: first, the lawyer, who is an expert in the Law of Moses, recites these two commandments as the greatest suggesting a larger rabbinic tradition, and second, that Jesus himself also refers to these directives in Mark as the greatest of the Law's commands, reveals that Jesus stands within the mainstream Judaism of his day.[11]

---

11 I am aware of the possibilities of redaction here in which one account is edited into the other making the speaker in each case different. Nevertheless, it is not impossible to consider that Jesus would have had these words on his lips during his ministry, and that someone would have responded to Jesus what would have been the obvious answer to his question. That both express the fundamental teaching of the Hebrew Scriptures and later rabbinic commentary is obvious. See I. Howard

The second major reason is that in Luke after the short conversation between Jesus and the lawyer, the narrative continues with the parable of the Good Samaritan (Luke 10:30-37) in which Jesus defines neighbor as all in need regardless of any specific ethnic standing. While the Law of Moses provided for strangers and aliens to be treated equally as Israelites (Exodus 12:49; Leviticus 19:33-34, 24:22, 27:19; Numbers 9:14, 15:15-16, 29: Deuteronomy 10:19), as is human nature, God's people in the Old Testament and in Jesus' day, privileged their own over others. When Jesus tells the parable of the Good Samaritan, he is not simply telling the lawyer to be kind to his own; he was expanding the definition of neighbor to include the enemy (cf. Matthew 5:43-4); for by the time of Jesus that is what Jews and Samaritans had become.[12] The punch of the story is not only received in Jesus' insistence that Jews help Samaritans, but that they be willing to receive help from Samaritans. There is little doubt that the typical Jewish stereotype of Samaritans cast them as incapable of such compassion.[13] The lawyer's question that leads to the story is clear: loving God and neighbor are displays of covenant faithfulness and holiness. Such faithfulness and holiness cannot be had without treating the enemy as a neighbor.

JAMES AND JOHN—LOVING NEIGHBOR BECAUSE OF LOVE FOR GOD

It has been made clear that loving God and neighbor are inextricably bound together and are necessary for the holy life to the place where both are assumed that one cannot be had without the other. Yet, two writers in the New Testament specifically highlight the necessity of keeping the two together, perhaps because the people to whom they write have found convenient ways to separate them. The letter of James, written by the brother of Jesus, and 1 John, which tradition assigns to the Apostle John, reinforce the

---

Marshall, *Commentary on Luke*. The New International Greek Testament Commentary (Grand Rapids: Eerdmans, 1979), pp. 440-441.

12 For a brief history of the Samaritans and their conflicts with Jews see *Ben Witherington, New Testament History: A Narrative Account.* (Grand Rapids: Baker Academic, 2001), pp. 189-192, 276.

13 We need to recognize that Samaritans had their stereotypes of Jews as well.

necessity of loving God and neighbor as faithfulness to the covenant reflecting holiness.[14]

In chapter three of James, the writer discusses the power of the tongue and the damaging effects words can have on others. The specific verse that speaks to our concern is 3:9, "With it [the tongue] we bless the Lord and Father, and with it we curse those who are made in the likeness of God." James reminds us of what is affirmed in the first book of the Bible. God made human beings in his divine image and they are to reflect that image by imaging God in the world. In Genesis 2:28 we read, "God blessed them, and said to them, "Be fruitful and multiply, and fill the earth and subdue it." A good conceptual translation of the Hebrew word for "subdue" is "put your stamp on it." Human beings are to stamp their image on the earth, which means they are to stamp God's image on it. James undoubtedly has Genesis in mind. How can God be blessed in one breath and then curse those made in the divine image in another breath both uttered by the same tongue? Holy speech cannot be had by praising God alone. To speak to or about someone in a way that no one would dare think of speaking to God demonstrates unholy character, even if the mouth that curses others sings praises to God in the most beautiful melody imaginable.

Just like James, John minces no words in his first letter.

> Whoever says, "I have come to know him," but does not obey his commands, is a liar, and in such a person the truth does not exist (1:4).
> For this is the message you have heard from the beginning, that we must love one another. We must not be like Cain who was from the evil one and murdered his brother (3:11-12).
> Those who say, "I love God," and hate their brothers or sisters, are liars; for those who do not love a brother or sister whom they have seen, cannot love God whom they have not seen" (4:20)

What some apparently want to separate, John brings together again. Love for God cannot be had without love for neighbor; and

---

14 For the matter of authorship of 1 John and James, see David A. deSilva, *An Introduction to the New Testament: Context, Methods, and Ministry Formation.* (Downers Grove: InterVarsity Press, 2004), 452-454, 814-819.

if holiness is our loving response to the God who loves us, then love for neighbor is a necessary part of the holiness package. The biblical writers provide us with no wiggle room on godly neighbor love.

5. Going on to Perfection or The Pursuit of Holiness Today

One person who had much to say about holiness of heart and life was the founder of Methodism (along with his brother, Charles), John Wesley. In fact, for Wesley holiness was the goal of salvation; but that goal cannot be had instantly. It took a lifetime of walking with God. One does not become instantly perfect in the moral sense, but one journeys toward that perfection. In order to highlight Wesley's theology of holiness, I will refer to his writings and a few of the hymns by his brother, Charles.

Holiness—Delighting in the Amazing Love of God

In the chorus of the hymn, "And Can It Be That I Should Gain," Charles Wesley writes, "Amazing love, how can it be that thou my God shouldst die for me?"[15] Wesley's understanding of holiness, just like the biblical writers, begins with the amazing love of God.

In his sermon entitled, "On Love," Wesley's understanding of love is deeply rooted in the Scriptures.

> The love which our Lord requires in all his followers, is the love of God and man; --of God, for his own, and of man, for God's sake. Now, what is it to love God, but to delight in him, to rejoice in his will, to desire continually to please him, to seek and find our happiness in him, and to thirst day and night for a fuller enjoyment of him.
>
> As to the measure of this love, our Lord hath clearly told us, "Thou shalt love the Lord thy God with all thy heart." Not that we are to love or delight in none but him: For he hath commanded us, not only to love our neighbor, that is, all men, as ourselves; -- to desire and pursue their happiness as sincerely and steadily as our own, -- but also to love many of his creatures in the strictest sense; to delight in them, to enjoy them: Only in such a manner and measure as we know and feel, not to

---

15 *The United Methodist Hymnal.* (Nashville: Abingdon Press, 1989), #363.

indispose but to prepare us for the enjoyment of Him. Thus, then, we are called to love God with all our heart.[16]

It is impossible to read these words and not hear clear echoes of the Scriptures we have discussed thus far. It is revealing to reflect upon the verbs Wesley uses in describing how Christians love God and neighbor.

In reference to God, Father John says we are to delight in the love of God. Loving God is not drudgery, it is not a chore. We take pleasure in our relationship with God because we truly love God. That does not mean love never involves difficult decisions or sacrifice; but it is that genuine love that leads us to do what love requires, not out of obligation, but out of the desire to please the one we love. That is why we rejoice in doing God's will. We know that God loves us and God always wills what is best for us, so we in turn rejoice in being obedient because, as Wesley says, we find our happiness in God. When Wesley uses the word "happiness" he does not mean a sentimental feeling alone. He has in mind what the ancient Greeks referred to as *eudaimonia*, which refers to all the ways in which human beings flourish. It includes what is best for humanity; it is what makes for the highest good. Thus, one cannot obtain this kind of happiness—*eudaimonia*—in selfish pursuits. A good Christian translation of the word is "blessedness." The Hebrew synonym might be *shalom*, which refers to a holistic peace that is individual and communal.

As Wesley continues in the quote above, he inextricably connects our love of God with neighbor. That happiness we receive in loving God is then turned toward the neighbor. As our love delights in God, so our love for neighbor leads us to delight in those around us, to see them as God imagers just as we image God to them.

But this love of God and others is not some abstract feeling with no implications for how we live. Many years ago, when I was in Haiti, the Christians I served with liked to say that love was an active verb. Wesley would no doubt agree. What it comes to how we love God and neighbor Father John is very specific. It is to this we now turn.

---

16 "On Love," Sermon 139, http://wesley.nnu.edu/john-wesley/the-sermons-of-john-wesley-1872-edition/sermon-139-on-love/

For John Wesley, doctrine was not a conversation on the theoretical. Theology was practical in nature. He referred to it as "practical divinity." Wesley's concern with doctrine was that, first and foremost, it assisted in shepherding God's people in holy living. This does not, mean as some have suggested, that Wesley was not a systematic theologian. It has been adequately demonstrated that Wesley thought systematically.[17] However, his theological writings are *ad hoc*, that is they are written to address specific matters for the people called Methodists. That Wesley wrote no systematic theology *per se*, should not lead us to conclude that Wesley was not a systematic thinker; but he rightfully understood that doctrine at its best was inherently practical and assisted the faithful in daily Christian living and witness. Wesley did not believe that talking holiness alone was sufficient. If holiness was our loving response to the God who loved us, then it must be shown in our love of neighbor. Holiness talk alone was hypocritical.

THE GENERAL RULES[18]

In 1743, John Wesley published The General Rules which were meant to guide the Methodist societies. "The Rules are a simple and concise description of basic Christian practices."[19] There are three.

First: *By doing no harm, by avoiding evil of every kind, especially that which is most generally practiced,* such as:

- The taking of the name of God in vain.

---

17 See Randy Maddox, "John Wesley – Practical Theologian?" *Wesleyan Theological Journal* 23 (1988): 122–47. Accessed at https://divinity. duke.edu/sites/divinity.duke.edu/files/documents/faculty-maddox/07_ John_Wesley-Practical_Theologian.pdf; Thomas C. Oden, *John Wesley's Teachings.* 4 Volumes (Grand Rapids: Zondervan, 2014). Oden's treatment of Wesley as a systematic thinker is the most complete treatment in print.

18 "The General Rules of the United Methodist Church." https://www.umc. org/en/content/the-general-rules-of-the-methodist-church.

19 Discipleship Ministries: The United Methodist Church "The General Rules." https://www.umcdiscipleship.org/resources/the-general-rules.

- The profaning the day of the Lord, either by doing ordinary work therein or by buying or selling.
- Drunkenness: buying or selling spirituous liquors, or drinking them, unless in cases of extreme necessity.
- Slaveholding; buying or selling slaves.
- Fighting, quarreling, brawling, brother going to law with brother; returning evil for evil, or railing for railing; the using many words in buying or selling.
- The buying or selling goods that have not paid the duty.
- The giving or taking things on usury—i.e., unlawful interest.
- Uncharitable or unprofitable conversation; particularly speaking evil of magistrates or of ministers.
- Doing to others as we would not they should do unto us.
- Doing what we know is not for the glory of God, as:
- The putting on of gold and costly apparel.
- The taking such diversions as cannot be used in the name of the Lord Jesus.
- The singing those songs, or reading those books, which do not tend to the knowledge or love of God.
- Softness and needless self-indulgence.
- Laying up treasure upon earth.
- Borrowing without a probability of paying; or taking up goods without a probability of paying for them.

Secondly: By doing good; by being in every kind merciful after their power; as they have opportunity, doing good of every possible sort, and, as far as possible, to all men:

- To their bodies, of the ability which God giveth, by giving food to the hungry, by clothing the naked, by visiting or helping them that are sick or in prison.
- To their souls, by instructing, reproving, or exhorting all we have any intercourse with; trampling under foot that enthusiastic doctrine[20] that "we are not to do good unless our hearts be free to it."

---

20 In Wesley's day, an enthusiast was someone who preached on the Holy Spirit and shunned the use of reason in Christianity. It is true that Wesley preached the former, but he did not support the latter.

- By doing good, especially to them that are of the household of faith or groaning so to be; employing them preferably to others; buying one of another, helping each other in business, and so much the more because the world will love its own and them only.
- By all possible diligence and frugality, that the gospel be not blamed.
- By running with patience the race which is set before them, denying themselves, and taking up their cross daily; submitting to bear the reproach of Christ, to be as the filth and offscouring of the world; and looking that men should say all manner of evil of them falsely, for the Lord's sake.

Thirdly: By attending upon all the ordinances of God,[21] such are:

- The public worship of God.
- The ministry of the Word, either read or expounded.
- The Supper of the Lord.
- Family and private prayer.
- Searching the Scriptures.
- Fasting or abstinence.

If one wants a picture of what holiness looks like in day to day living, this is it.

As one looks down the specifics of each General Rule, there are things that seem strange to our ears. We no longer buy and sell slaves (Thank God!) but holiness demands that we treat all people as made in God's image. Others in the list may surprise us, particularly the admonitions to live simply and frugally. The list Wesley created was specific for his day, though I think it can be said that most of what he enumerates is still applicable today.

---

21 Bishop Reuben Job's conceptual rewording of the Third General Rule as "Stay in love with God," has become popular, but is, in my view, unfortunate. Living in a context where love is over-sentimentalized, particularly when "in" is added, undermines the practical and communal context of the ordinances Wesley had in mind. The phrase by itself is problematic. See Rueben P. Job, *Three Simple Rules: A Wesleyan Way of Living* (Nashville: Abingdon, 2007).

Three things should be noted here in looking at these lists: First, the way of holiness is rigorous and can be difficult. Holiness should not be rejected because we find it too trying, nor should holiness be watered down into an ethic of just being nice. Second, for Wesley holiness was not simply a private matter in which we spend our days at spiritual navel-gazing in reading Scripture only by ourselves, praying only by ourselves, and doing nice things for people by ourselves. Such personal time and action are important in the pursuit of holiness, but in our individualistic world where me, myself, and I are what matter most, it must be said that holiness of heart and life has an intrinsically communal component. In order to clarify both, we finish with Wesley's understanding of the Sermon on the Mount. Third, we must always be diligent that keeping any code of conduct does not become the end in and over itself. When the focus on any rule is on keeping the rule alone and not a means to the end of loving our neighbor, then we become more like the Pharisees and less like Jesus.

6. Discipleship in the Current Age

John Wesley believed the Sermon on the Mount was very relevant for the current age. Of his fifty-two standard sermons, thirteen are from texts on the Sermon on the Mount. Wesley says several things in his first sermon from Matthew 5:1-4. (All the following quotes are from this sermon.)[22]

First, Wesley suggests that Jesus' teaching in Matthew 5-7 focus on showing the way to heaven. He says this not only from the context of the Sermon, but because of the one preaching it—"From the character of the Speaker, we are well assured that he hath declared the full and perfect will of God." The character of the one proclaiming means that the words spoken are "true and right concerning all things." Wesley is placing the Sermon in the larger Nicene-Chalcedonian theological context. Jesus' words are true and right because the one speaking the words is divine.

Second, Wesley clearly rejects any suggestion that the Sermon on the Mount was meant only for the current generation of people to whom the words were originally spoken, nor are they words meant only for future generations in an eschatological context. The sermon was meant for "all the children of men; the whole race of mankind; the children that were yet unborn; all the generations to come, even to the end of the world...." He offers the following reasons for his contention.

1. If Jesus had meant the teaching to be only for his twelve apostles, he would not have preached this sermon publicly and on a mountain. A private home would have been sufficient. When Matthew says that the crowd gathered and his disciples came to them and Jesus began to teach them, "them" does not refer only to the Twelve, but to the entire crowd that gathered to listen.

2. The words of the Sermon itself make it clear that Jesus was preaching to everyone. Wesley writes, "No man, for instance, denies that what is said of poverty of spirit relates to all mankind." How is it, for example, that only some of Jesus' followers are to be the salt of the earth and the light of the world? How can it be that

22 John Wesley, "Upon Our Lord's Sermon On the Mount: Discourse One, (Sermon 21) https://johnwesleysermons.com/sermons/upon-our-lords-sermon-on-the-mount-discourse-one/.

only a future generation of disciples can be guilty of murder in their hearts or commit adultery in their lusts? For Wesley, the very character of Jesus' instructions makes it clear that these are words meant for all disciples for all times and places.

There appears to be some confusion in Wesley's first sermon on Matthew 5-7 when he insists that these words are for "all mankind." Does he mean all persons, even those who are not disciples? That could be the case depending upon how one interprets his words, "all the children of men; the whole race of mankind," but yet Wesley's exposition of the Sermon also seems to suggest the requirement of Christian conversion. For example, he states,

> Some have supposed that he designed, in these [the Beat-itudes], to point out the several stages of the Christian course; the steps which a Christian successively takes in his journey to the promised land;-- others, that all the particulars here set down belong at all times to every Christian. And why may we not allow both the one and the other?

3. The Sermon on the Mount for Wesley is indeed Christian morality. He observes of Matthew 5-7 that "Christianity begins just where heathen morality ends." There is a decisive and, in some cases, unique character to Jesus' instruction. Wesley notes, for example, that when it comes to poverty of spirit "the whole Roman language... does not afford so much as a name for humility."

It is this decisive character of the Sermon on the Mount that forms the church to be a city set on a hill. And for Wesley, that light is to shine from Jesus' followers in every generation. That light is holiness of heart and life.

7. CONCLUSION: HOLINESS IS IRRESISTIBLE

In conclusion, we return to the book of Isaiah.

> In the year that King Uzziah died, I saw the Lord sitting on a throne, high and lofty; and the hem of his robe filled the temple. Seraphs were in attendance above him; each had six wings: with two they covered their faces, and with two they covered their feet, and with two they flew. And one called to another and said:
> 'Holy, holy, holy is the LORD of hosts;
> the whole earth is full of his glory.'
> The pivots on the thresholds shook at the voices of those who called, and the house filled with smoke. And I said: 'Woe is me! I am lost, for I am a man of unclean lips, and I live among a people of unclean lips; yet my eyes have seen the King, the LORD of hosts!' (Isaiah 6:1-5).

Isaiah not only witnesses the grandeur of God, but God's holiness as well. In the world of the ancient Near East, the word "holy" was not extensively used, and it was a word that had no moral connotations. When Israel's neighbors used the term "holy" to describe their deities, they were simply affirming that their gods were not common. But for the Israelites, the notion of God as holy was very different. God's holiness not only meant that he was different from human beings, but that he was morally superior to human beings. His character was perfect and his actions were always just.

As Isaiah stands in the presence of this holy God, he realizes, perhaps as never before, that he is anything but holy. "Woe to me!" Isaiah shouts. "I am ruined! For I am a man of unclean lips, and I live among a people of unclean lips, and my eyes have seen the King, the LORD Almighty."

We are an unclean lot, and as Isaiah is enveloped in the presence of divine holiness, he knows he is a sinner. Yet, this truth is not only confined to the prophet; it is true of God's people as well. Perhaps in the presence of the holy, Isaiah believes that God will now destroy him. But Isaiah underestimates the grace of God. God will send upon him, not the fire of destruction, but the fire of purification. "Then one of the seraphs flew to me with a hot coal in his hand, which he had taken with tongs from the altar. With it, he touched my mouth and said, 'See, this has touched your lips; your guilt is taken away and your sin atoned for.'"

Isaiah is made holy. Holiness is necessary so that others can see the character of God in us and in his people. Holiness is our loving response to the God who first loved us. There are those who think quite negatively about holiness. Some believe holiness means walking around looking as if one has been sucking on sour lemons. Others believe that holiness means a life of boredom. But as that great Christian thinker C.S. Lewis writes, "How little people know who think that holiness is dull. When one meets the real thing, it is irresistible."[23]

---

23 C.S. Lewis, *Letters to an American Lady* (Grand Rapids: Eerdmans, Reissued 2014), p. 27.

Topical Line Drives

Straight to the point in 44 pages
https://topicallinedrives.com

www.ingramcontent.com/pod-product-compliance
Lightning Source LLC
Chambersburg PA
CBHW010039040426
42331CB00037B/3332